The
Bushes

by
Cass R. Sandak

CRESTWOOD HOUSE
New York

Maxwell Macmillan Canada
Toronto

Maxwell Macmillan International
New York Oxford Singapore Sydney

Library of Congress Cataloging-in-Publication Data
Sandak, Cass R.
 The Bushes / by Cass R. Sandak. — 1st ed.
  p. cm. — (First families)
 Includes bibliographical references (p.) and index.
 Summary: An account of the life of George Bush and his family, with emphasis on his years as president.
 ISBN 0-89686-632-7
  1. Bush, George, 1924– —Family—Juvenile literature. 2. Bush, Barbara, 1925– —Juvenile literature. 3. Bush
family—Juvenile literature. 4. Presidents—United States—Biography—Juvenile literature. 5. Presidents—United
States—Wives—Biography—Juvenile literature. [1. Bush, George, 1924– . 2. Presidents. 3. Bush, Barbara,
1925– . 4. First ladies.] I. Title. II. Series: Sandak, Cass R. First families.
E882.S26   1991
973.928'092—dc20
[B]   91-11153
                                                                                                                    CIP
                                                                                                                     AC

Photo Credits
Photos courtesy of AP—Wide World Photos.

CRESTWOOD HOUSE

Macmillan Publishing Company   Maxwell Macmillan Canada, Inc.
866 Third Avenue   1200 Eglinton Avenue East
New York, NY 10022   Suite 200
                                    Don Mills, Ontario M3C 3N1

Macmillan Publishing Company is part of the Maxwell Communication Group of Companies.

Produced by Flying Fish Studio

Printed in the United States of America

First edition

10 9 8 7 6 5 4 3 2 1

CONTENTS

President Bush discusses the Gulf War with Defense Secretary Richard Cheney (left) *and General Colin Powell* (right).

Bush's Toughest Moment

In August of 1990 Iraq's Saddam Hussein annexed neighboring Kuwait. The world rose in protest. Hussein ignored a United Nations demand for withdrawal of troops from Kuwait by January 15, 1991. The next day President George Bush authorized a force of U.S. bombing missions to destroy Iraqi weapons stockpiled in that country.

The world watched and waited as full-scale war unfolded on TV screens the world over. And everyone, it seemed, waited for answers. The questions most asked: How would the war and the decision to fight it affect George Bush? And what kind of war was it going to be? Would it be a short-term air war? Or would ground fighting cause the war to last for many months?

As it turned out, the war in the Persian Gulf was a great military success. It was known by the name Operation Desert Storm. The nation had rallied behind President Bush and his tough decision to wage war.

The war was over six weeks after it started. Saddam Hussein's forces had been driven from Kuwait. The coalition forces had perfomed their task swiftly and effectively. And there had been a minimum of casualties among U.S. troops. Pride in the country and its military might were at an all-time high. And Bush's popularity soared.

Bush has often wondered about history's assessment of his presidency. One of his campaign slogans was READY TO BE PRESIDENT FROM DAY ONE.

Another great president, Abraham Lincoln, is one of Bush's heroes. Bush has said of the president who preserved the Union through the Civil War: "He was tested by fire." The same can be said of George Bush.

President Bush in the Oval Office with members of his senior staff shortly after announcing a cease-fire in the war against Iraq.

Five-year-old George with his sister, Nancy, in 1929

Young George

George Bush was born in Milton, Massachusetts, on June 12, 1924. Bush's father was Prescott Bush, Sr., a successful businessman. Originally from Columbus, Ohio, the elder Bush was a partner in an investment banking firm. The president's mother, Dorothy Walker Bush, came from St. Louis, Missouri. They had been married in Kennebunkport, Maine, in 1921.

George has an older brother, Prescott, Jr., or Pres. Pres is two years older than George. His other brothers and sister are John, William (Bucky), and Nancy.

George Bush has written that his father instilled in him the "old-fashioned idea that the more advantages a man has, the greater his obligation to do public service."

Prescott Bush was a Yale graduate who had served in World War I. In 1950, at age 55, Prescott Bush decided on a career in public service. He ran for senator from Connecticut. He lost by a narrow margin, but when the incumbent died in 1952, Prescott Bush was nominated to replace him. In a special election, Bush won the Senate seat. Prescott Bush served in the U.S. Senate for ten years.

George Bush grew up in Greenwich, Connecticut, a wealthy suburb located about an hour's drive from New York City. The family's rambling, dark-shingled Victorian house was in the Deer Park neighborhood. At the house, the Bushes had three maids.

George credits his parents with serving as role models—the children admired them and wanted to grow up to be like them. They raised the family with love and discipline. The Bushes, staunch Episcopalians, regularly attended Christ Church in Greenwich. The family had daily Bible readings around the breakfast table. These readings included discussions of Jesus' parables and their application to daily life.

George was known as Little Pop or Poppy after his grandfather Walker, who was known as Pop. When he was two years old, George's parents briefly called him "Have Half." This was because he always wanted to share his toys and possessions with his older brother, Prescott.

When George was a young boy, family Christmases were spent on a plantation called Duncannon. This South Carolina estate was owned by his grandfather Walker.

George (left) with brother Prescott, Jr.

There the family shot quail and doves, and rode and hunted on horseback. The house was warmed by great pine logs roaring in the fireplaces.

But the Bushes spent as much time as possible at their house in Maine. The family home in Kennebunkport is called Walker's Point. It had been purchased by Bush's grandfather and his father as a vacation home. Tennis and golf were favorite sports. Sailing and boating were also popular with the family.

Long walks along the rugged beach and forays in the family fishing boat have always been part of the Bushes' relaxed way of life at the retreat. When George was nine, his grandfather let him man the estate's lobster boat all by himself. George's eleven-year-old brother, Prescott, kept watch. Being in control is the place George Bush likes to be.

Young George Bush, along with Prescott, attended Greenwich Country Day School. Then George went on to Phillips Andover Academy. At Andover the boys were preoccupied with news of World War II. Their classroom studies were supplemented by first-aid training and courses in radio and signaling. George excelled in his studies, as well as in sports and student activities.

When George graduated from Phillips Andover in 1942, the commencement address was given by Henry Stimson, Franklin D. Roosevelt's secretary of war. A trustee at Andover, Stimson was to become a particular hero of young George's.

George at War

George had planned to go to college after graduating from the academy. But the United States had recently entered the war. So in 1942, on his 18th birthday, George Bush enlisted in the naval flight program. When he received his wings, Bush became the youngest pilot in the U.S. Navy.

Bush named his Grumman Avenger torpedo bomber Barbara, after a girl he had just met. The aircraft carried a payload of four 500-pound bombs.

Bush served as a fighter pilot in the Pacific. He was shot down by a Japanese anti-aircraft unit in September 1944. When Bush was shot down, he was on a bombing mission against a radio-transmitting station on Chichi Jima, a Japanese-controlled island. Chichi Jima is part of the island chain that includes Iwo Jima, the famous battle site. Bush had just flown over the communications tower when the Japanese guns opened fire. He dropped his loads of bombs and headed out to sea. The two crewmen flying with him bailed out before the plane hit the water, but they were never found.

Other American pilots, still airborne, helped protect Bush as he floated in the sea. They were able to point out his life raft drifting nearby. Another pilot dropped him a medical kit. But Bush's only injury was a gash on his forehead. A fellow pilot, Doug West, was in another plane. He machine-gunned an enemy boat and drove it away. This gave Bush the chance to swim to his life raft. Bush was rescued in mid-ocean by an American submarine, the USS *Finback*.

Because of this and his flight record, Bush was awarded the Distinguished Flying Cross for bravery in action.

11

World War II navy pilot George Bush in the cockpit of his plane, Barbara III

Barbara Pierce Bush's graduation photo from Ashley Hall

Barbara Growing Up

Barbara Pierce had a privileged and happy childhood in Rye, New York. Born on June 8, 1925, she is the daughter of Marvin and Pauline Pierce. She is the great-great-grand-niece of President Franklin Pierce, but the family has modestly never said much about this connection.

Marvin Pierce was a publishing executive, the president of McCall Corporation. The company publishes, among other things, women's magazines. Perhaps because of this, the Pierces were always a family of readers.

When she was 16, a high school junior, Barbara was sent to an exclusive boarding school in Charleston, South Carolina, called Ashley Hall. There she was recognized as a serious student, and she particularly excelled in drama.

She was at home from school during Christmas vacation in 1941. At a dance she attended, Barbara Pierce met George Bush. Bush was still a senior at Phillips Andover. Barbara was only 16. And the United States had just entered World War II.

Barbara describes George as the first man she ever kissed. A year and a half later George and Barbara became engaged. The Bushes were such a young-looking couple that George asked Barbara to lie about her age! They kept their engagement a secret from everyone but their families. George Bush was about to go off to war as a navy fighter pilot.

After logging a total of 58 combat missions, George was given leave to return home. When he got to Greenwich on Christmas Eve in 1944, Barbara had already dropped out of Smith College during the fall of her sophomore year.

The Bushes' wedding was originally planned for December 19. But George didn't arrive home until Christmas Eve, so the wedding was rescheduled for January 6, 1945. Oddly enough, George and Martha Washington had been married on the same date, but nearly 200 years earlier.

George wore his navy dress blues for the ceremony. After the wedding at Rye's First Presbyterian Church, the newlyweds celebrated at a reception for more than 250 friends and relatives at a nearby country club. The great reunion was a welcome time of relaxation and joy in the midst of a war that was still months from being over.

After World War II

The newlyweds were stationed at Virginia Beach, Virginia, when victory was declared in August 1945. The navy saw to it that the young pilot's discharge papers were processed promptly. In September George entered Yale University in New Haven, Connecticut.

When George Bush enrolled at Yale in the fall of 1945, he joined the largest freshman class in the school's history. Normally about a thousand new students enter each year. That year, however, the freshman class numbered 8,000. Of these, some 5,000 were returning servicemen.

At Yale Bush played varsity baseball. And in 1948 he was first baseman and captain of the Yale baseball team. During the same season the team won the NCAA Eastern regional championship. Bush got to meet baseball legend Babe Ruth, who had come to New Haven to give a manuscript to the university library.

By 1948 George had to juggle several roles. He was an athlete as well as a student. He was also a husband and a father. George and Barbara's first child, George Junior, was born in July 1946. Despite all his activities, George was a good student. He finished a four-year course in three years and was elected to Phi Beta Kappa, the national fraternity that honors scholastic achievement. He majored in economics and graduated with honors in June 1948.

Soon after George graduated, the Bushes moved to Texas. There George Bush wanted to build a career in the oil business.

George Bush in uniform as captain of the 1948 Yale varsity baseball team

15

A young George Bush in flight gear. He never wanted a conventional kind of life.

Years of war experience followed by the period at Yale had convinced Bush that he didn't want a predictable and conventional sort of life. He didn't want to work for the family investment firm. He wanted the opportunity to make it on his own. He briefly considered a career in farming but then decided on oil. The Bushes set off in the summer of 1948, in a Studebaker that had been a graduation gift from George's father. They also had $3,000 in cash that George had saved from his navy pay. It wasn't much, but it was enough.

Bush had first visited Texas as a navy pilot. He was intrigued by the rough-and-tumble way of life, by the oil industry, and by the prospect of working hard and getting rich.

And where better to succeed in oil than in Texas, the center of America's oil industry. The Bushes' first home in Odessa, Texas, was a duplex. One half was the Bushes' while the other half was a whorehouse. Bush started out working in the oil industry as an equipment and sales trainee, earning just $375 a month.

From Odessa, Texas, the Bushes soon moved to Midland. In between, they spent a short time based in California. When the Bushes moved to Midland, it had a population of only 25,000. Today it is a city of close to 100,000. There Bush set up his first business, with John Overbey, a neighbor. The 26-year-old Bush and his partner developed oil fields all over the West—as far as Montana. Within a few years they had added two partners.

By 1956, when Bush was 32, he was made president and chief executive officer of the oil company that he and Overbey had founded. The firm took its name, Zapata, from a Marlon Brando film about a Mexican hero. The partners had just seen the film. Ten years later, in 1966, George sold his share of Zapata to devote himself full-time to politics.

Life was good to the Bushes in Texas. They rode the oil boom of the 1950s and became financially successful as a result of hard work and long hours. By the early sixties, Bush was a wealthy man. He had achieved what he'd set out to do. It was now time to consider what he might be able to do in public service.

A Career in Politics

Bush followed in his father's footsteps when he decided on a political career. Bush first campaigned for public office in 1964. He ran for the U.S. Senate. Two bids for a Senate seat failed. But in 1966 Bush found himself elected to the House of Representatives from Houston's 7th District. In this capacity he served two terms. He earned a good reputation as a strong congressman. He also made plenty of political contacts in Houston and in Washington.

Barbara and George at the polls in 1964. This was the President's first campaign for public office, when he ran, unsuccessfully, for a Senate seat.

As U.S. Ambassador to the United Nations, George meets with President Richard Nixon, Henry Kissinger (left) *and William Rogers* (center).

Bush then came to the notice of President Richard Nixon. He was appointed to a succession of high-level positions. He was named U.S. Ambassador to the United Nations and served from 1971 to 1973. This was Bush's first post of international importance. He took to it well and showed great powers as a mediator. During this time Bush was able to witness the workings of the international community and to become familiar with world leaders. During his term the People's Republic of China was admitted to the United Nations. Another of Bush's responsibilities was to work on U.S. policy regarding Arab-Israeli relations.

At Nixon's request, Bush became chairman of the Republican National Committee in 1973. Now he was able to focus on the political scene in the United States. In June 1972 the Watergate break-in had occurred. Bush attempted to hold the Republican party together during the period following the Watergate scandal.

President Nixon resigned in 1974 in the wake of Watergate. His successor, Gerald Ford, offered George Bush the choice of ambassadorships to Great Britain or to France. But Bush turned down both offers. Shortly after, Ford named Bush to a new post. Between 1974 and 1975 Bush was chief of the U.S. Liaison Office in China.

During their 15 months in China, the Bushes threw themselves into the unfamiliar and ancient culture. George and Barbara developed a deep understanding and appreciation of Chinese art, food and life. The Bushes endeared themselves to the people of Beijing by traveling around the city on their bicycles, as the Chinese themselves do. Only occasionally did they use the special car and driver that had been placed at their disposal. The Chinese affectionately referred to them as "the Bushers."

President Ford called Bush home from China in 1975 for a very special job. Bush went to Langley, Virginia, for two years as director of the Central Intelligence Agency. While head of the CIA, he oversaw American intelligence efforts on a worldwide scale. He also saw the agency regain much of its prestige and credibility. Both had been seriously undermined during the Vietnam War.

In 1980 Bush lost the Republican nomination for the presidency to Ronald Reagan. But Reagan was very impressed with Bush's record. So Reagan chose him as his vice presidential running mate. In large measure, Bush is actually indebted to Gerald Ford. Ford declined the honor just 24 hours before Reagan offered it to Bush.

Vice President George Bush holds talks with a Chinese delegation. Bush has worked to improve relations between the United States and China.

George Bush being sworn in as vice president of the United States by Supreme Court Justice Potter Stewart

Bush as Vice President

Ronald Reagan won the 1980 presidential election handsomely. And in January 1981 George Bush was sworn in as vice president of the United States.

On two occasions, Bush came close to being named president. The first was when an attempt was made on Reagan's life in 1981. Some years later, on July 13, 1985,

Bush *was* actually named acting president for several hours. This was done because Reagan was about to undergo surgery. A special congressional act provided for Bush to step in if something went wrong. In both cases, no further steps were necessary.

The office of vice president of the United States has always been hard to define. The vice president's only official duty is as presiding officer of the Senate. But under Reagan, the vice president's role was strengthened somewhat.

As vice president, Bush oversaw several important domestic programs. Reagan asked Bush to head the National Security Council's special crisis-management team. Task forces dealing with crime, drugs and illegal immigration took up much of the vice president's time.

Bush also had a good deal of experience in foreign policy, while Reagan had little. This made the vice president's role extremely important. Even though Reagan and Bush were not close personally, Bush came to be regarded as one of Reagan's top advisers.

The president also showed his reliance on Bush by making him the chief spokesperson for the economic policies of the Reagan administration. Unfortunately, the results of most of these policies have come back to haunt George Bush today. The wild prosperity some people experienced in the eighties was counterbalanced by increased poverty and desperation for others. The collapse of many financial institutions, the mounting national deficit, and the recession of the early nineties are all legacies of Reaganomics.

To the White House

George Bush is only the second person named George to have become president. This happened during the 200th anniversary year of the American presidency. George Washington's election, by the electoral college, had occurred just 200 years before.

George Bush's election victory of 1988 was the third in a line of three consecutive presidential terms by Republicans. This was the first time that had happened in more than 50 years. The last time was in 1928. However, only 91 million voters turned out. It was one of the lowest voter turnouts in nearly half a century. Almost the same number of eligible voters stayed home.

President and Mrs. Bush with Vice President Dan Quayle and his wife, Marilyn, at an inauguration party

George dances with Barbara at one of the nine inaugural balls held in their honor.

January 18, 1989, was Bush's Inauguration Day. Early that morning the Bushes and most of the family attended services at St. John's Church on Lafayette Square in the nation's capital. Later that day Bush was sworn in as the nation's 41st president. He used the same Bible that had been used by George Washington!

After the inaugural ceremony, the Bushes attended many parties. The first stop, however, was at the Lincoln Memorial, which signaled the beginning of the inauguration festivities.

In the evening the Bushes circulated among the nine inaugural balls held in their honor at various locations around the nation's capital. One of the largest balls was for 5,000 people. It was held in Washington's recently restored Union Station. This elaborate cavern of a building is the capital's main railroad station.

On the morning after the inauguration, the president was already at work, and Barbara led a tour group through her new home.

Barbara always has time in her busy schedule to play tennis, to swim and to do needlepoint. She is well organized and highly disciplined. Barbara always finishes what she starts. She always thanks people for gifts or kindnesses. Usually she handwrites thoughtful thank-you notes and letters.

George Bush is also a considerate correspondent. In a hallway outside the Oval Office he has had a small storeroom converted into a tiny private office. The room is equipped with a desk and typewriter. Here Bush bangs out brief notes of congratulations, thanks or words of encouragement. Lest anyone think he farms out this duty to any of his staff of secretaries or assistants, he always includes the words "self-typed" near his signature.

The down-to-earth, unassuming Barbara Bush came to the White House as the best-traveled presidential wife ever. Before becoming first lady, she had accompanied her husband on trips to 68 countries and had clocked over 1.3 million miles. This experience has given her a broad knowledge of world affairs and world problems. It also means that she had already met almost every world leader before she became first lady.

Barbara Bush had moved 29 times in 44 years of marriage. When she and George Bush moved into the White House in 1989, it made their 30th move!

The new first family. As president, Bush approached the world's most powerful post with a feeling of serenity.

The First Family

The Bush clan is large and close-knit. They gather frequently for family events. The first family may get together at the White House. Or they may meet at the comfortable, rambling house that looks out over the ocean in Kennebunkport, Maine. There they enjoy swimming and boating, among other relaxations. There they may also entertain world leaders.

The Bushes with some of their many children and grandchildren

George and Barbara, with granddaughter Ellie LeBlond, wave to a crowd while viewing a Memorial Day parade in Kennebunkport, Maine.

The Kennebunkport house is the Bushes' official home. It is filled with mementos from more than three-quarters of a century. It also holds memories of long summer afternoons spent catching starfish in tidal pools and clambering over the rocks of the rugged Maine coast.

George and Barbara Bush have five grown children. They are George, John (or Jeb), Neil, Marvin and Dorothy.

Like most children, each one had his or her challenges while growing up. Young George had to overcome the burden of having the same name as his dynamic father. Neil's childhood problems included a reading disability, while Jeb had difficulty growing up in a competitive family. Marvin had a series of childhood illnesses, and Dorothy was painfully shy.

The Bushes have 12 grandchildren, whom they call "the Grands." The younger grandchildren refer to the president and Mrs. Bush as Gampy and Ganny.

In the summer of 1990 Dorothy Bush LeBlond separated from her husband. She moved from Cape Elizabeth, Maine, to Washington to be near her parents. She took three-year-old Ellie and six-year-old Sam with her.

Son Neil has frequently been in the public eye. He has ties with the threatened savings and loan industry. And there is some indication that not all these ties have been honorable ones.

There was another child, a daughter, Pauline, known as Robin. She died of leukemia when only three years old. Her months of illness and her death were among the most difficult challenges the Bushes have had to face.

Barbara Bush is a strong person in her own right. Her manner is warm and relaxed. She seems able to put everyone at ease. She herself has stated that she looks like "everybody's grandmother." And she is also a remarkably witty and perceptive woman. Few are safe from her barbed humor. In her family she is known for her quips and for her ability to mimic just about anybody. She has even been known to impersonate Soviet leader Mikhail Gorbachev.

Barbara admires one of Millie's puppies during a benefit for Reading Is Fundamental, a literacy program supported by the first lady.

Millie wants to play ball with Barbara during a White House press conference.

The first lady aroused considerable controversy when she was invited to return to Smith College, as the Class of 1989's commencement speaker. Many of Smith's feminists questioned Mrs. Bush's credentials as a role model for young women. After all, she had chosen to leave Smith in her sophomore year to become a housewife and mother rather than a career woman. Still, Mrs. Bush was able to turn the occasion into a triumph.

Mrs. Bush's address held her audience—as well as listeners around the country—spellbound. She justified the decision she had made early in life. She said that life's regrets stem not from missed business opportunities but from failing to give enough time and attention to family and friends. The humane focus of her talk hit home and won new fans for the first lady among men and women of all ages.

Soon after moving to the White House, Mrs. Bush was diagnosed as having Graves' disease. This is a disorder that causes the thyroid gland to overwork. The problem at first caused her eyes to protrude. She lost over 20 pounds—and two dress sizes. Beyond that, the disease has not been a major inconvenience and is being controlled by drugs. Mrs. Bush is philosophical about the problem. She is the first to state that it is "not a great adversity."

Barbara's white hair is one of her most striking features. She started to turn gray prematurely when she was still in her 20s. She dresses simply and wears costume jewelry. Her fake pearls have become legendary. Mrs. Bush sums up her popularity by saying that people know "I'm fair and I like children and I adore my husband."

The president owes at least some of his success to Barbara's hard work. She may not be the typical political wife, but she is an excellent one. She seems really to care about people.

Prominent houseguests have been impressed by the open affection that the Bushes display for each other. They show a genuine interest in each other's activities. But this interest still leaves plenty of room for independence.

George Bush and Soviet leader Mikhail Gorbachev play horseshoes at Camp David as their wives look on.

Bush as President

In the first years of Bush's presidency, world events underwent radical changes. In the Soviet Union a movement toward freedom and *glasnost* (openness) under Mikhail Gorbachev changed the whole international scene. The Berlin Wall was taken down, marking the end of a divided Germany. Communism came under threat from dissatisfied people who had lived too long with it.

But George Bush had little or no impact on these events. In fact, for a long time Bush has had to fight a "wimpy" image. Many see him as overeducated and overprivileged. He is not a charismatic speaker. At best, his voice is apt to sound whiny. When he is tired or preoccupied, he tends to stammer. Bush has tried to overcome these liabilities.

One of Bush's first foreign-policy crises came early in his administration. In 1989 the Chinese government clamped down on student protesters. The name Tiananmen Square suddenly was known the world over. Some students were killed there and many were injured. For a time it looked as if a new Chinese civil war might be erupting.

And the Middle East has been a source of anxiety for Bush and his advisers. The aggression of Iraq's Saddam Hussein as well as the unresolved Israel-Palestine issue have both been major challenges for the administration.

In January each year *Time* magazine names a single figure as its man of the year. In 1991 the magazine changed its tactics. It named one person *men* of the year.

That person? George Bush. The reason? Because, according to *Time*, Bush really has two points of view. His very strong global vision is balanced against a less effective grasp of the domestic scene.

MEN OF THE YEAR

TIME

The Two
George Bushes

George Bush on the cover of Time

Only days after that issue of *Time* magazine appeared, Bush's global strategy was put to a severe test. He faced his toughest challenge when he set the United States on the road to war with Iraq on January 17, 1991. With the successful end of the war in only six weeks, Bush's popularity among the American people skyrocketed.

The domestic issues still have to be attacked. Among the key problems that Bush faces are drug abuse, homelessness, education, race relations and the environment. But some feel he does not have much of a grasp of these issues. And many believe that conditions have actually worsened in the United States during his administration.

The Bushes fill out their 1990 family census form.

Barbara watches Millie and her newborn puppies on the White House lawn.

A Day at the White House

Barbara Bush promised herself that even as first lady she would continue to lead a normal life. The Bushes wake around six A.M. to country music sounding from a battered clock radio they have had for years. Usually George then flips through the TV channels, studying the news programs. Typically, Mrs. Bush leaps out of bed, throws on some clothes, and rushes to the White House lawn with her dog Millie. Often she will then return to bed to enjoy a cup of coffee before tackling the day's challenges.

There the Bushes pore over newspapers, marking and reading aloud items of interest. As they read, they fortify themselves with fruit juice and coffee.

By seven A.M. the president is dressed and headed for the Oval Office. First on his agenda are up-to-the-minute briefings with his advisers. These briefings usually last until shortly after nine in the morning. Meetings are often held with his chief of staff, John Sununu, or with cabinet members.

The president's own time begins after nine A.M. Then he controls the schedule. He often meets with members of Congress and with lobbyists (representatives of special-interest groups). Courtesy calls from old friends or celebrities passing through Washington take up part of most mornings.

Barbara's own office is upstairs in the East Wing. From there she can look out her window and see George working at his desk in the Oval Office.

A pleasant dining room for the chief executive's own use has been made out of the office of a former aide. Here the president entertains friends at relaxed luncheons. Invitations to lunch with the president may be issued as late as half an hour before noon. Barbara usually lunches with friends upstairs in the family's private living quarters.

The Bushes are not always careful about what they eat: french fries, onion rings, sirloin steak and cheesecake rank high among their list of favorite foods. The Bushes also serve and drink alcohol when they entertain, but not to excess. They try to make a point of eating out in restaurants about once a month.

The president's favorite dishes range from Peking duck to snails in garlic butter. Almost 40 years of living in Texas has given all the Bushes a liking for Tex-Mex food. They are fond of cheese enchiladas especially, and the hotter the better. Bush does not like foods from the cabbage family, especially broccoli and brussels sprouts.

George Bush is 6 feet 2 inches tall and keeps his weight a trim 195 pounds. He has blue eyes and brown hair. He is the fourth president to be left-handed.

Exercise is a regular part of the Bush routine. Two or three times a week he runs two miles. He used to do five miles, but he is taking better care of his battered knees these days. He also uses a treadmill and an exercise bike. And the president has been known to pitch horseshoes on the White House lawn.

An avid sportsman, Bush takes an afternoon jog after playing a round of golf.

In May of 1991, Bush was hospitalized briefly. Doctors found an irregular heartbeat caused by an overactive thyroid gland. The condition reponded to medical treatment and the president resumed his active life. Now it appears that Bush as well as his wife is suffering from Graves' Disease.

Barbara Bush is also an active person. She enjoys a brisk walk, a game of tennis or a swim. In early 1991 her activity led to an accident. She broke a leg while sledding with her grandchildren.

And once, while swimming in the White House pool, she saw a large rat swimming alongside her. Her screams brought help from her husband, who drowned the intruder with a pool scoop.

Barbara tries her hand at pool at a neighborhood recreation center.

The first lady reads to a group of day-care students at the Library of Congress to celebrate the 1989 Year of the Young Reader.

The Bushes are a reading family. George Bush likes nothing better than to read a few pages of a mystery or suspense novel at night in bed before falling asleep.

And Barbara has a long-standing interest in literacy. During the years her husband was vice president she made more than 500 appearances at events related to literacy programs. This was in addition to some 130 other appearances she made on behalf of many volunteer programs. The first lady is currently honorary chairperson of the Barbara Bush Foundation for Family Literacy.

The Bushes usually call it a day about ten P.M. Any informal entertaining they do is usually over by this time. Millie gets one last walk with one or both of the Bushes.

The Bushes' English springer spaniel Millie became a media heroine when she gave birth to a litter of puppies in 1989. The puppies were born in the private White House beauty parlor. In 1990 a book "by Millie" became an instant best-seller. The book looks at life in the White House from a dog's point of view.

41

The Bushes say their prayers aloud at night. But the president admits that, more often than not, they say them lying in bed rather than on their knees. Both believe in the power of prayer. Barbara, especially, says it is good to pray because it focuses your thoughts on trying to do better.

The Bushes frequently retreat to Camp David. It is a presidential getaway a few miles from Washington. Situated on Catoctin Mountain, the site has been a weekend home for presidents since the time of Franklin D. Roosevelt. In fact, the Bushes drew some criticism because they spent the first weekend following the beginning of the Gulf War at Camp David. Many Americans thought they should have remained at home during this tense time. But no one could doubt the president's sincerity and his belief that the war in the Persian Gulf was the right course of action. The evangelist Billy Graham spent the night following the start of the war with the Bushes at the White House, praying with them and advising them.

President Bush stretches out after jogging with the White House dogs, Ranger and Millie.

Barbara points the way back to the White House after she and Millie see the president off on a trip.

A Life on the Go

The Bushes have long led an active life. Their lifestyle combines both Texas and Northeastern viewpoints. Their experience makes them especially well equipped to deal with the complexities of world leadership.

At the same time, the Bushes cultivate an image of Middle America with dogs, pork rinds, barbecues and hunting parties. Two of Bush's favorite actors are movie stars of the forties: Clark Gable and James Stewart. They seem to symbolize ideals of commitment as well as cool detachment. President Bush likes to think of himself as competent and in control, self-reliant and ready for whatever may come.

The Bushes have always worked on volunteer projects to benefit minorities. During the Yale years, both George and Barbara gave their time to raise money for the United Negro College Fund. From an early speech, the phrase "a thousand points of light" has remained. It means that individuals who volunteer *can* make a difference in improving social conditions.

The Bushes have drawn some criticism because they come from privileged backgrounds. They also have been accused of being insensitive to the needs of the working class and to middle-class people, to say nothing of the poor and homeless.

When Bush came to the presidency in 1989, he looked upon the office as an exciting personal challenge as well as a chance to be of service. He approached the world's most powerful post with a feeling of serenity. A Bush adviser was echoing the president's own words when he said that Bush "intends to enjoy this in the manner of Teddy Roosevelt, not treat it as some dreary drudgery."

It will be many years before historians are able to judge the Bush presidency. George Bush dreamed of a new order in Europe. He saw it reach fruition in the late 1980s with the collapse of communism in Eastern Europe, the unification of West and East Germany, and the liberalization of the Soviet Union. Whether his vision of a new order for the world holds together remains to be seen.

The President holds one of Millie's first puppies.

For Further Reading

Buchman, Dian Dincin. *Our 41st President, George Bush.* New York: Scholastic Books, 1989.

Bush, George, with Victor Gold. *Looking Forward: An Autobiography.* New York: Doubleday & Co., 1987.

Friedel, Frank. *The Presidents of the United States of America.* Revised edition. Washington, D.C.: The White House Historical Association, 1989.

King, Nicholas. *George Bush. A Biography.* New York: Dodd, Mead and Company, 1980.

Klapthor, Margaret Brown. *The First Ladies.* Revised edition. Washington, D.C.: The White House Historical Association, 1989.

Radcliffe, Donnie. *Simply Barbara Bush.* New York: Warner Books, 1989.

St. George, Judith. *The White House: Cornerstone of a Nation.* New York: G. P. Putnam's Sons, 1990.

Sufrin, Mark. *George Bush, The Forty-first President of the United States.* New York: Delacorte Press, 1989.

Sullivan, George. *George Bush.* Englewood Cliffs, NJ: Julian Messner, 1989.

NOTE: Because the Bushes are in the news all the time, newspapers, periodicals and television news programs are also major sources of information about them.

Index